We
Alive,
Beloved

We Alive, Beloved

FREDERICK JOSEPH

Row House Publishing recognizes that the power of justice-centered storytelling isn't a phenomenon; it is essential for progress. We believe in equity and activism, and that books—and the culture around them—have the potential to transform the universal conversation around what it means to be human.

Part of honoring that conversation is protecting the intellectual property of authors. Reproducing any portion of this book (except for the use of short quotations for review purposes) without the expressed written permission of the copyright owner(s) is strictly prohibited. Submit all requests for usage to rights@ rowhousepublishing.com.

Thank you for being an important part of the conversation and holding sacred the critical work of our authors.

Library of Congress Cataloging-in-Publication Data
Available Upon Request
ISBN 978-1-955905-64-0 (TP)
ISBN TK (eBook)
Printed in the United States
Distributed by Simon & Schuster
First edition
10 9 8 7 6 5 4 3 2 1

Contents

III.

IV.

V.

These are merely tools used by sensitive men to carve out a piece of beauty or truth that they hope may lead to peace and salvation.

—GIL SCOTT-HERON

I.

Notes from Therapy

This world bruises us into retreat.
A half-life crawling back to the womb, away
From false starts and things we have been.
But in the house of becoming there are no clocks—
No chimes marking transformation—
Only the whisper of possibility. An expanse
Vibrating in the palm of your hand.
Choices shaped like rivers endlessly branching its waters.
Begin in your life's timid daybreak
Or begin in the twilight of your years.
Our lives are a gallery of unfinished portraits.
Each stroke—a choice. Unrestrained, untamed
By the leash of time, each breath, each moment,
A fresh parchment. Write, rewrite, until the ink runs dry.
Let it startle you. Become a sunburst
In a winter sky, laughter in a room of silent faces,
Become raindrops tracing veins
Of a leaf, or unexpected ballads in city noise.

Making Luxury Out of Flat Soda

I learned to breathe in my grandmother's kitchen
despite life sitting on my chest.
Scent of cast-iron skillets seasoned by sunrises
and ancestors' hands. Gospels of sizzling grease
and bubbling greens my uncle called hallelujah and amen.

Wallpaper aged like the wrinkled hands of generations
sitting at her table arguing over cards
and gossiping over cognac. Grandmommy's kitchen
where on shattered days, when the world was crumbling
and she forged forward
with the pennies and dust America gave her,
I learned to draw maps through life's pitfalls.

Grandmommy's kitchen had soul but I wished for luxuries,
like my classmate's kitchens, like sitcom kitchens,
like kitchens that fed kids not worried about light bills.

In the aisles of the unwanted, she bought soda gone stale.
Labeled with a bargain's grace, flat as the depleted smile
of a penny-pinching survivor. But in her hands,
the deserted became an idea—a diamond for joy's crown.
In the bowels of her humble freezer
that soda surrendered to cold's gentle grasp.
My maker of miracles—a humble alchemist—
transformed the unimpressive into glimmers
gifting us something more than survival.

With a whirring blender creating a symphony of ingenuity
flat soda became a slushie—a frost-kissed wonder.
Luxury birthed from the discarded.
More than a frozen treat, she shared a philosophy:
a lesson in how to breathe in more life than you've been given.

Clay

For Michael Latt

I want more for us
Than a tally of missteps
Than ragged white flags
Worn by the winds of regret
Battered by our worst moments
I want a life as monuments
Not of past failures
But of work to become
A story to pass down
Not merely a relic weathered
In remorse nor a fossil of our broken
Promises and lost faith
For us I dream of clay
Ready for form from which
Old faults are stretched into beauty

On Days I Am Dying

I find just enough reason to breathe
in a Frank Ocean song.
Looping lyrics stitch a lifeline
to the parts of me sinking into silence.

Artists can be a buoy,
tethered to tomorrow,
uncoiling the sorrow
knotted in the throat.
Each chord, a conversation
with the void, fleeting declarations
of promise written
in rhythms whispering *you're not alone.*

Songs, like mirrors,
reflect my fragments,
painting portraits in shades
of experiences that stare back at me.
In a stranger's lyrics, there are letters
addressed to me,
postmarked from dawn.
A voice with eyes
that hold pain I know too well, yet
it's the survival that is contagious.

Him: Tender

Is laughter until our abs hurt the reclamation
Of humanity? Should we find out? This way, brother.
Between the lines of their definition for masculine
Where we chuckle like children until our cheeks hurt,
Build each other up until our hands are calloused,
Voices rasp from being honest about our wounds.
In the wisdom of our tears, we remember old language—
Vulnerably stitching together a bridge to healing.
Or, if you need, we can just sit here and be silent.

As a Boy, I Watched Westerns

Wading through the gravel of endless prairies alone
yearning for the taste of gunsmoke in my mouth.
The far-off glare of sunsets on the horizon,
held in my vision like the answer to every question I asked

alone as I watched how they made my uncles spark
like flintstones under the broad expanse of a technicolor sky.
Leaving them in awe of the lonesome desert
swallowed within the glass belly of a television,
leathered skinned, lone horseman strays, finding themselves
among the dust of life's hardship, with no friends other than
their faithful horse and their even more faithful rifle.

This is all he needs when the world is settling
on his broad shoulders like the slow birth of mountains.
Randall, Butch, Mark, my three desperadoes,
coming and going, never resting or staying too long.

These men of mine, like tumbleweeds on a Sergio Leone
    canvas.
They would laugh with gruff voices like worn cowhide
and smelled of saloons and a trail of broken hearts.

I'd sit on the edge of my childhood, legs too short to touch
    ground,
in slippers I pretended were weathered boots, perched on a
hardwood stool that some might have mistaken for
a plastic covered couch, memorizing those rugged reels of
    fiction.

Holding them between us as a lifeline. Believing in the
    screen's
amber glow, I might find a language to bridge
the gulfs that spread vast and silent between our generations.

I needed to know their language, to have the desert
on my tongue, to see the world through cigarette-creased eyes,
to find my place with them on the new frontier. So I could be
    seen
by someone who could teach me to be a man, too.

Rivers of Time

As it loops and tangles,
Shimmering like sequins in the sun,
Perhaps time is but a bead of water
Dripping, merging, vanishing into unknown rivers.
All I am sure of is that if ours ran its course,
I would unmake the universe, vast and unyielding,
Amidst the dance of a billion lives,
So that it might be reformed in the image
Of us resounding—again.

Session I: Learning to Speak

I was an adult when I began the difficult labor of speech.
In the gray light of a stranger's office grew a wasteland of
  words
Catacombs of hidden hurts, of joys too fragile
To share, stubborn in my throat. Voice trembling like a
  newborn's cry.
Each syllable, an act of creation, each silence, a statement of
  intent.

"Where should we start?"

Well—I'm Black, in a time where just being
Black isn't marginalized enough. Disabled, but not enough
for most to care. Fatherless, but I don't tell people
to avoid tropes. Mother-less when it matters,
even when everyone says "She's still your mom." Depressed,
but who isn't these days, so I never
bring it up. Engulfed by trauma, not knowing
whether I'm a good husband. Riddled with anxiety,
wondering what being a good father looks like.
Questioning myself about the extent of my writing
talent, if I have any. Oh, and, the potential of being
poor again constantly over my head, like a cartoon anvil
that falls out of nowhere.

"How about we start at the beginning."

Between my teeth, the syllables shivered, nestled like unlit
    candles,
But he could see my stories were refugees: uprooted and lost,
Seeking sanctuary. Silence stirred like tea leaves, eyes with
    notes
Of a brewing storm. Before lips can know language,
The heart must know truth.

How strange it feels to bloom so late, after wearing disguises,
To camouflage in crowds, and in myself. But to speak at all
Is to be right on time—at least that's what my therapist said.
As my tongue stumbled over the debris of dread, relinquishing
The paper fortress of loss, I sculpted sentences out of my
    sorrow.

With each word an island is born, rising from an ocean of
    unbroken
Self, fortified under the therapist's gaze, each nod
Of understanding becomes a grain of sand gathered until
there is land enough to inhabit: a continent of voice.

The Lasso Way

I'm unsure whether white people are redeemable,
but every so often Ted looked like something else.
I know my history, just as well as I know his,
carving the world's skin with the edge of privilege,
drowning us in his delusions of grandeur,
colonizing our bodies with manifest destiny.

Digging for gold in the depths of Black souls.
There are times when I'm a good Black person,
thus, I never lost sight of his true form.
God dammit if I don't be smiling, though.

White privilege is knowing the recipe for kindness and
    disaster,
and choosing the latter so much I hate myself for grinning,
or finding my reflection in the softness of a Midwestern drawl
that probably sounded like my ancestors' worst fear in a
    mustache
that reminds me of every man who nearly took my life.

I hate the idea of white people making me ponder
or melt when climate change is their fault.
So are the rest of my problems.
God dammit if I don't be smiling, though.

Gosh, if white manhood is an absent theater, tucked under
    shadows
looking to fill itself, what if instead of bones it chose laughter?

When I realized I was giving Ted more humanity than he'd
    given me,
my Black became disappointed. Skin recoiling until I
    remembered
the names they gave us.

I'm unsure whether white people are redeemable,
or if Ted just found a new mask in a closet full of white robes.
God dammit if I don't be smiling, though.

Cereal Time Machine

I eat a bowl of cereal every week to help me stay alive.
Not for sustenance, but to defy time.
A communion with the parts of me time tried to vanquish.

Swaying as I chew, I hear dreams once had:
Thoughts of dancing on the moon's face.
Imagining myself on a stage singing to thousands of fireflies.
Ballads in Saturday morning jingles and theme songs.
An undying selfhood in spoonfuls of reachable tomorrows.

The rebellion of adolescence reborn in each bite.
This porcelain roundness contains my fragments,
So, I will try to swallow myself whole again.

Legacy Born in Ash

I have watched rivers turn skeletal beneath an atomic sun,
Seen forests laid low and undone in the throes of
Merciless wildfires set by no one and everyone.
I've choked on smoke-blackened skies
Bruising cerulean until they're gray
Palms smeared in the grit of a home in peril.

Still, each night, I rock the dream of an unborn child
And wake with the excitement of an unfinished poem.

Then, in a voice weighted by day's gravity, I ask the mirror—
Could I invite a little one into this, a world
Unraveling like old wool in indifferent hands?

Maybe it's vanity. Trying to exorcise the ghosts
Left by a father I never knew,
Mother whom I haven't seen in years.

Am I wrong for wanting to christen a child with a name
Drawn from the wellspring of our ancestors,
Gift them laughter from my favorite movies,
Pass down the colors of teams I cherish,
Show up for them in the places I felt alone?

Could I bear the weight of a child's trust broken,
Knowing there was a way to protect them from it all?
As I yearn to press my own life into another,
I know evergreen love cannot be an everlasting shield
For Black children still living as both miracle and target.

Pillow Talk

In the veiled language of moonlight, I have made love to
   shadows,
negotiated with the gravity of time unraveling my secrets.
The pearls of years I'll never know again—seventeen and
   twenty-three.
Seventeen, when first kisses tasted like summer rain.
Twenty-one, when I stumbled from dim-lit bars into lust.
Like murmurs against the shell of memory, now elusive.
I have bathed in the dense wild of sunrise,
questioned the love that braids itself around my heart,
unnamed, untamed. An erratic flame kindling upon the
   unknown.
A constant question mark in the book of my life, unmarked,
unhinged. But once, when I dreamt of climbing mountains,
and traveling to different planets, I woke up and you were still
   there.
Crumpled under the blanket of darkness. Words were empty,
so, it was quiet. What is this feeling? I've never worn this
   before,
I don't even know its name. Are we but another flicker,
   momentary
pixels in the grand unfolding of oblivion? When the sun rose,
you were gone, leaving stardust on my pillow. Left
hoping you don't misplace me, like you did your girlhood
   crush,
like you did thirty and twenty-three.

II.

For the Good Times

For Thelma Ford

Grief is like a house
With no doors, only mirrors
Existing in the unlit corners,
Where a grandmother's love is now just a name,
And moments with her grandson are now just stories.
It sits on your shoulders
With the weight of a cold voice
Letting you know the cancer won.
While its foundations sink deep within,
Waiting to remind you she's gone,
Veiled in Al Green's music.
Echoing in her kitchen's soft glow,
Each note, a love letter, each lyric, a sigh.
Stranding the two of you on different sides.
On one, she might still be dancing,
The other, you're packing up things she left behind.
Asking how do you place yourself in a cardboard box,
Without tears bursting it open
Whenever you find her voice,
Neatly tucked into her favorite songs?

I, Sorry, Mother

Don't weep for us, Mama.

Save what little
you have left.

Withhold your rivers,
settle your aching heart,
as we slaughter sobbing forests.

Please, Mama. Rest your voice.

Save your sermons
of fish wallowing in black waters
and birds plummeting from shattered skies.

For in ivory towers built to scrape heavens,
the congregation prays only to profits.

Until we no longer poison your tears,
do not weep for us, Mama.

A Marriage Story

How many times have we been strangers in our shared home,

parallel bodies passing like ghost-ships in the sea of our bed?

Sparking wildfire from language, the violence of words

hurled in haste, in hurt, becomes weapons of mass destruction.

Voices hoarse from shouting, hands trembling

with the weight of grievances. *"Then leave!"*

I have known the arc of your resentment,

as intimately as my conversations with God.

In the depths of your laughter I ask, *What is love,*

if not the greatest of paradoxes? We go to war with no enemy,

but there are casualties everywhere. Marriage makes many

    sounds—

sometimes it's the slamming of doors, or the sigh of

    frustration,

sometimes it's the sweetness of our names upon each other's

    lips.

It's the hush of our souls folding back toward home, in a

    whisper

of welcome back. *"You want to watch something?"*

A Black Man's Smile

In memoriam:
Stephen Laurel "tWitch" Boss 1982–2022
Kalief Browder 1993–2015

I always show teeth
Less for myself
And more for you
I am not afforded luxuries
Of tears, weariness, scowls
For what shelter is there
For the Black man
Less than a cardboard box
For the Black boy
When storms rage and winds howl
We achingly ask the ocean
Do you cry when you see us drown?

I Don't Read Reviews

Monday, 9:03 AM
Subject: Your Recent Review on "Blackity Black: A Book for
    Black Folks"

Dear Brad,
In the dimmed dawn of your critique,
where every word casts its shade
over my soul's endeavor, I ask: Is it the narrative
or the prism through which you gaze
that blurs the image?

Those pages are more than ink and paper;
they are diasporic heartbeats, rhythms, blues,
tragedy and triumph you've yet to comprehend.

It is a cruel thing, to judge a song by notes
your ear cannot catch. Did you review my book,
or did you review the scope of your own understanding?

❖

Wednesday, 11:57 AM
Subject: Re: Your Recent Review on "Blackity Black: A Book
    for Black Folks"

Malik,
Isn't it critique's purpose to pen what I perceive?
Your narrative, its song,
shrieks in ways my ears will not follow.

If story is penned for all then should it not embrace all?

Is it not a writer's duty to bring everyone along
regardless of race?

❖

Wednesday, 12:15 PM
Subject: RE: Re: Your Recent Review on "Blackity Black: A
    Book for Black Folks"

Dear Brad,
It's not the embrace I question,
but the complexion of the arms
being asked to wrap around the words.

Can the moon truly fathom the sun's blaze?
Your review reflects the limits of your lens
not the reach of my story.

My work that bears the weight
of your misunderstanding.

In every word I write, there is fresh water
for all who are parched.
But if all you see is that I have given food,
because you are also hungry,
or you only crave honeyed milk,
do you blame the sky
for not raining your desires?

❖

Friday, 5:06 PM
Subject: Re: RE: Re: Your Recent Review on "Blackity Black:
   A Book for Black Folks"

Malik,
Again, in my realm, I critique what I see.
Your waters, however distant, should beckon me
all the same. Perhaps the lake you penned
should have reflected something more
vast and suited for my scope.

In the end, whose job is it to free me
of my supposed limits?
Why should one apologize for not seeing
what could have been better shown?

❖

Friday, 5:42 PM
Subject: RE: Re: RE: Re: Your Recent Review on "Blackity
   Black: A Book for Black Folks"

Dear Brad,
Limits—indeed.

Unless you have ever tasted a history so vibrant
it clings to your tongue, how can you judge me?

In this case, it's not the stars that falter. If every word was
   written

only for ears attuned to familiar rhythms,
how quietly singular our world would be.

My prose is the language of my heritage,
not riddles to be unraveled. Your review flutters
like uncertain feet on unfamiliar soil,
and I think, perhaps, you did not walk far enough
to see where I'm coming from.

Your Eyes Don't See Me

You see me as a stranger. Am I intruder
Or wearily asking for direction? You don't see
Me as family. Though I was born right here.
Next to innocent you—
Next to not-so-innocent you.
Though you've no semblance of my name.

Like you, I am part 1619 and 1776.
There is also 9/11 in me.
I have watched, as you've chosen
What we should never forget
And what truths your children needn't know.

In 2020, my body came into vision,
But not my name, not what wakes me,
Not what has kept me alive.

You still see me as a tool. Am I teacher
Or Magical Negro guiding fragility? You don't see me
As family. Though you believe otherwise.

When you do, you will know my name—
Twisted in the edges of America's tongue.
Carried on the winds of stories woven into my skin,
Of dancing nights away, sharing moonlit kisses,
And walking barefoot to feel our home between my toes.

2012 Nights

A river rages against the jagged cliffs of my larynx,
teetering on the edge of my tongue like welling tears.
Not here. Not now. Not ever.
I was Tamir Rice's age when they let me know,
my anger is not mine to have. My sorrow
ain't neither. Shit—sometimes my laughter becomes theirs too.
I've been housing a thousand silent screams
since I was about George Stinney's age.
My throat, a crypt for buried typhoons,
hushed, a life of muted thunder
until I find raging brown seas
in half-empty bottles of whiskey. Washing away
the doctor's diagnosis. *Multiple Sclerosis.*
Am I washing away?
How do I handle this and Trayvon Martin?
I'm sleeping on people's couch,
and my student loans due, and nobody hiring a nigga,
and me and mom ain't on speaking terms
again, and I scream until my throat is raw,
my heart is throbbing, my chest is heaving, my ribs
untwine, bones no longer wound like a second
spine, and I am empty.
The world trembles at my pain.
I scream until I cry,
and will cry until I am human again.
Every wound is a word, and every scar is a verse
echoing over the bottle shattering on the wall.

On the Annual Day of Fireworks

Why should I celebrate a nation
Where tomorrow remains a coin toss?
Knowing not whether that sound
Means I should run and hide
Or wonder at the sky.

The Odyssey

Suicide is the third leading cause of death for Black men ages fifteen through twenty-four. That number is steadily climbing.

I. Black Boy

Beneath the heavens of false gods, a Black boy rises.
His existence, a single flame, dances in grandiose ebony.
His gaze, obsidian dreams, cradles the yet-to-be,
etched in the verses of a destined odyssey.
His hands, tender vessels of promise, clutch a butterfly
    midswoop,
crafting dreams into champions, knuckles up, eyes aflame,
and hearts that thunder against the artistry of his mind.

Fingertips stained with the wisdom of soil,
naivete adorns his moments as earthen delicacies.
Still, the world peers, cautious, predatory,
seeing only the imagined marks his touch might create.
A forecast birthed from murmurings and specters
cast onto the canvas of his not stroked existence.

Pallid gazes, harboring cyclones,
lay assault to the innocence of his movements.
Outline his shape: a red strike
against their ledger of dread and incomprehension.
His very core twisted into a judgment, a decree,
penned even before the ink has touched parchment.
A quiet encroachment, this, the gradual hemorrhage of a tale
not of his crafting, seeping into the weave of a skewed society.

Yet the Black boy, oh, his grin persists,
his joy's radiance casting light into the darkest corners.
Misunderstood, true, for now,
are the carvings of intolerance and venom
that loom in the lifeblood the child passes down.
His smile resounds, a tune meandering
through the institutional mazes and out into light.

For within this Black boy, a lighthouse rages,
a defiance—an unwavering tenacity.

II. Black Threat

Our Black boy evolves, stretched by the years

into a striking portrait of adolescence.

His voice, now layered with the resonance

of a thousand histories,

tells of Liberia and plantations, of Mansa Musa and crack,

each word a waterfall cascading over the precipice of silence.
His stride, a testament to Jay-Z's bars and Singleton's camera.
He is a lighthouse, his spirit cutting a path through the fog,
yet the world insists on casting him in shadow,
framing the luminance of his smile as a cloud of fear.

They see him, yet they do not see him.
They misinterpret his energy for life.
They label him "talkative" then "too much" then "thug,"

seeing only the few hours before midnight of his skin,
and jealous of the galaxies beneath.

A society, steeped like bitter tea in fear,
bathes in the falsehood of Black as synonymous with wrong.
In their minds, melanin is a marker of menace,
a twisted signal fire of a threat existing only in perception.

Yet he remembers how to crawl, and learns to claw,
finding his way out of the storms of his city.
Unwavering against the gales of this unforgiving world,
his spirit refused to bow to their hurricanes.

His spine steeled by the pieces around that offer dignity,
a bridge connecting the sacrifices made
to the promise of a future his elders foretold.
The Black teenager lives, despite their disappointment;
his war cry roars as he heads to battle, despite their lies.

III. Black Dick

To the wilds of America's godlessness, the Black
young man, his mind and passion reduced
to profit margins, his body reduced
to glutton's misguided desires. Each muscle,
curve, thought, becomes a fantasy for others,
their hunger gnawing at the edge of his soul.

His worth, appraised in crass currencies,
stripped of his essence, his complexity,
he becomes a token to be traded on the block,

a spectacle painted into the corners of exploitation.
Robbed of his depth, he's placed in distorting light,
squeezed of humanity, folded into their pockets.

Oh, how they all gaze, but hers are truly something,
her jungle fever thrills and mandingo cravings
cast their skyscraper shadows over his form.
Nauseating chisels chips away at his personhood,
molding him into an erotica book chapter.

Weapons, cunning and merciless, wielded against dignity,
turning his very presence into an internal battlefield,
where his identity grapples with crude caricatures
allowing himself to become a prop in their theater.
He has lost himself in the bowels of his story.

Yet somewhere beneath those catacombs,
the true Black young man remains caged, his mind hungry.
His dignity intact, refusing to be shed at the whims of others.
He stands firm, a fortress against the blue-eyed onslaught.

His gaze, a mirror, reflects their halfness,
shaking away the facades projected on him.
The Black young man stands, remembering
the worlds under skin, he is unbroken,
he is radiant, he is who we had hoped for.

Despite their cruel attempts to encase him in phallus molds,
he shines, illuminating the truth of his being—
a young man of profound wholeness.

IV. Black Identity Extremist

From the arena of turmoil, a man rises,
chanting for justice, crying out for an end to the cruelty.
He stands: a monolith in the sea of black shirts,
his desperation cutting through the apathy of privilege,
his voice an awakening, for those who didn't care,
that he had been dying right beside them this entire time.

For kinfolk fallen, a tear trickles down the cheek of time,
a fist clenches in shared pain, a sequoia grows in defiance.
Each child lost fuels a fiery scream, an elegy pulsating
in the heart. Billie Holiday's blues, ignored by a rhythm-
    stealing nation.

The world watches, a spotlight on his determination,
its ear tuned to the sound of his march cracking concrete.
His story engulfed in tear gas, his hope bloodied by baton,
marks of the beast like a rite of Black passage.

He is more than a living mosaic of pain and disproportion,
each piece its own dimension of multitudes,
shimmering in the light of Black gold, the strongest
known substance, as veins bloom on his forehead,
AIN'T I A MAN?! He bellows down the halls of the FBI,
NYPD, and Supreme Court. *AIN'T I A MAN?!*

Yet they deny him still as three-fifths, even the "good ones,"
his pleas for justice labeled as divisive, he is again "too much."
They fear his words, not their truth, but the mirror
they hold to their complicity, their benefit.

His existence becomes an unsettling reminder of their sins,
a call to action too loud for their comfort.
Yet he does not waver, for he knows
that their supposed unity, if built on the silence of the
    oppressed,
will be but a veneer over the chasms of injustice.
Filled with the bones of victims of their hunger.

The man stands firm, but his losses are many. Time. Joy.
    Oxygen.
He knows the road is paved with ashes of those who faced
    more,
but he doesn't want to be a martyr, he just wants to grow old.
Sadly, that desire sounds like anarchy to those feasting
On his spirit. Somehow, he persists, bearing the weight of
    truth,
to those who will listen, illuminating the path to something
    more.
But they want so much and do so little.
His mind, his heart, his time, his freedom, his perfection.
They claim they want to break his chains,
but they merely paint them in other shades of alabaster.

V. Black Escapist

Ain't I . . . a man? He has spent his years questioning,
in a mirror that seems to have more lies than answers.

Our Black man has been dreaming of freedom less,
though the tree still stands. He desires sleep above all else.
They have handed out too many death sentences,

while no longer wanting to discuss his body being a
    battlefield,
they have all the selfies they need while the Target store burns.
His struggle a fleeting trend. His humanity a fad.
"Sorry, I won't go viral for trying to be John Brown."

He yearns for a haven untouched by it all,
a sanctuary unscarred by the sword and savagery,
a place unmarred by the necessity of code-switching fear.
Where he is not the burden they said his great-grandfather
    was,
as they hung him from a tree he planted and placed him
on a postcard. *Is there even a soul left to be saved?*

One day, in the stillness of a morning he wished he could gift
to those who were taken without knowing peace,
he finds not despair but the wind carrying poetry of what's
    next.
He will take it all: glances, scrutiny, blows. So it might become
a verse in the tale of his last life because this can't be it:
an ode to the Black body being stretched in the false world.

He escapes. Not from his skin, but from his ache,
delving into the possibility of what comes next.
Finding solace in his darkness, comfort in its depth,
remembering the galaxies he contains. *I'll go there one day!*

He wants nothing more than to fold into himself,
frolicking through the vast expanse of a Black boy's dreams,

swirling nebulas where there is still milk and honey.
They won't be able to hurt me there.

What he seeks, rather, is a bed, where he might smile
in his slumber, far from the twisted lens
through which he is perceived.
Almost where he is meant to be.

When the day finally arrives, whether our Black man is gray
    or not,
and the false gods have taken what they want and don't need.
They will look upon him with brimstone and curiosity.
"Why does he still smile?"
Then, in his last breath, the image of our Black boy returns.

You thought you had taken everything,
but we leave with all we came.

Forearm Thunderstorms

In the hazy light of an old dive bar—
a sudden lightning—a map
of thunderstorms. This was the first time
I read your silent warfare.

That thin pale thread of a tale,
jaggedly etched into your forearm:
a frayed whisper against supple skin.
It spoke of a night too heavy,
sorrow that tugged too often,
mornings always too dusk.

Your story was neither mine to ask nor tell,
so I tried my best not to stare.
My wandering eyes betrayed me.

You caught my gaze, raised your glass
to the scar, to the moment, to life.
Those eyes, deep wells of history,
spoke volumes in their quiet.

Then you whispered,
"We all have our stories."
Ice clinking against your glass.
"Proof you can survive anything."

What I Can Offer

Is a universe
Shaped in belonging
Not in consumption
Already teeming with life
With space for yours as well
To arrive and depart
As comfortably as you exhale

We Cry Together

Her shriek is raw, snapping all the world's quiet
As dreams, unborn, tumble into the abyss of almost.
I don't know this sound—an anguish that pierces my soul.
With what little strength I have, I grab her hand,
Weaving through the grooves of her sorrow,
Though my grip is frail.

The geography of her face is foreign to me
As the doctor explains the terrain of a pain
I cannot mend. A black hole I cannot save her from.
Nah, this can't be right. Look again! Refusing to accept my
    wife's body
As the site of such an inexplicable vanishing—
A promise left lingering in the world of daydreams.
She asks me and the doctor to leave the room,
Needing a moment to plead with the universe.

From the hallway, I hear her sobbing, an ocean devouring her
    smile.
My knuckles meet the steel door of a sterile hospital room,
Attempting to punch away our misfortune, until I can replace
    it
With something she actually deserves. For all of the IVF
    shots,
The nights we debated over names, the anxiety attacks about
    money,
And the moments we pinched ourselves at the idea of being
    chosen
by Saadiq. *Saadiq Joseph.*

How do you stitch a wound living in the syllables of a name
    never called?

There is nothing to say when spun into a vortex of
    unspeakable loss.
We spend weeks huddled around grief like a campfire,
Telling silent ghost stories about the people we stopped being
Just days before. Nurturing a flame so small it could be
    mistaken
for hope.

In the most somber hours, when the world took its deepest
    breath,
I sat beside her, staring at the slight crescent of her unhoused
    belly,
For so long, I swore I heard a heartbeat, but it was actually
    planets collapsing
In the cavities of my chest. And I wondered, how are we going
    to survive this,
And in time, my question was answered:
Together.

III.

Session II: You Still Try

In the belly of your heaviest days
Shadows dance as if they swallowed the sun.
When trauma's ghosts threaten to erase desires you penciled
   in,
And heartache makes a home in the marrow of your bones,
Sit with me, so we might hold a séance to resurrect your joy.
Let's trace a map of our existence,
Invisible routes inked in the language of survivors.
Our scars are not catacombs
but star clusters, bridging nights to dawn.
How do we make sense of it all?

Listen to the stubborn hum of our heartbeats.
Like oak trees choked by a storm,
with limbs bent and bark ragged—
you are still here.
Among glass shards of disappointment, in the throes
of loss and mausoleums built of regrets,
nestled deep in the trenches of daily tragedies,
you still dream. You still try.

See how you have weathered tantrums of grief and agony,
those wild children, biting and clawing,
leaving welts upon your soul that bloom into resilience.
Your hands are not the remnants of ruin—
they are star-kissed, constellation-etched,
each line a proud declaration, each callus a song:
We alive, beloved.

Because I Am Too Immense

to be consumed.
I am here. This morning.

Feet descend from my bed,
each toe, like a budding flower,
crashes to floor
with a thunderous
boom.

Sound of a force to be reckoned with
planted in my mother's garden.

Free Trade

I was on a beach before our greed-colored failures
Were all washed away by the ocean of time.
I just want to sleep a bit longer.
You were there, too, in the arms of the sun,
Stripped bare of green paper and metallic tongues.
No one could remember the anxiety of clinking coins.

Imagine the world afloat on an unbottled sea,
Where rat races do not wear us threadbare,
Uncarved by need and the cost of being born.

The earth beneath our feet, not a prize to be seized,
But a friend to know. Unfettered, unburdened,
We were young again.

The lemons of capitalism lost their rinds,
Peeled away into nothingness. A world free.

In the absence of profit, houses stood
As homes, not investments. We looked up
As the sky stopped billing us for its blue,
And the stars for guiding us home.

Do you remember? We were children once,
Tossing pebbles in streams, bartering them
For amusement instead of survival.

Learning to Be Single
from Dr. Manhattan

The door shuts, and in the infinite splinter of a second,
I unweave myself, and there is no noise.

I have seen galaxies be born and die within a single tear,
Felt the pulse of quasars and comets unravel in the palm of
    my hand.
Even when in front of her, I stretch into unimaginable
    tomorrows.
I become the observer, knowing loneliness is but the shadow
Of perception, and isolation a witness to existence.

\To be alone is not to be empty, it is to be all-encompassing,
A panoramic presence weaving around the sphere of time.
She is gone, but she is also still here. Just as I am now, and
    then.
We will spend eternity together, filled with me watching
Her laugh, cry, scream, want more, and leave.

\Here, where space bends its spine against the weight of
    unseen worlds,
I have found solace in solitude's magnificent choir, singing
In the key of infinity. I am a garden of silence, my thoughts a
    mirror,
Held up to the universe, a display in grandeur of the
    unknown.

O quiet, my celestial refrain, you are not the void,
But the realization that emptiness is but the bassinet of
    creation,
A haven for atoms to dance, planets to pirouette, stars to
    dream.
All around me now, I can hear the cosmic chorus whisper–
You are here, you are there, you simply are.

\In being alone, I am held aloof, by the gravity
Of my own consciousness, worried not that she is gone
To the arms of time, but rather the arms of someone else.

Survivor's Remorse

What a transgression, this breath,
Black person, daring to be more
than Black body, hashtag, pleaful sign,
plucked from the jaws of a street where
they said everything withers.

On my tongue, the taste of a full fridge.
In my palm, more thread count than callus.

But in my new neighborhood,
we don't have Black people.
When we do, they call us "are you sure you live here?"

Leaves me missing my old neighborhood,
where we didn't have white people,
and when we did, we called them "the cops" or "CPS."

My Father's Void

The ink had not dried on my birth certificate
when my father's form became vacant.
Casualties of Reagan's war on Blackness.
A cradle left to be rocked by echoes,
of sirens and fleeing footsteps.
Gone not as a thief, stealthy and kind,
rather as smoke dissipates, abandoning the fire.

But with his ghost, he left me
An inheritance. Not a void, rather a container—
A black hole. On the other side is me.
Pulling in fragments of cosmos,
From every soul who leans in close,
pouring into me parts of themselves
as hugs. Kisses. Laughter. Shoulders to cry on.

In the black hole my father left,
the vast expanse of that darkened space,
stars were born from every tear I shed.
I learned the dance of resilience, feet bare,
On the shards of what he could not give
I arose, clear and rare. Whole.

We Dance, Because We Alive

Before our feet were bound by leather and lace,
before our hands were filled with smartphones and bills,
we held the beat of the earth. When the world was still
young, and we were younger still,
we danced, until our feet ached, then danced even more.

[There is an anticipatory hush among the audience. The dancer steps forward, shadows parting. The spotlight finds them, bathing their body in a glow. They take a deep breath, letting the air fill their lungs, and exhale slowly, letting themselves fill the room.]

As they begin, contours of their silhouette hint
at journeys taken and yet-to-be embarked upon. The rise and
    fall
of their chest, the act of breathing, becomes a shared rhythm
    with the music.
Their feet trace patterns on the floor, each step a language
known by heart. The tempo quickens, the narrative evident—
this is a story of the heart's yearning, of battles fought within,
of agony, of whispered dreams, of flamboyant survival.
The dancer leaps. It's a flight of freedom, a burst
of joy. It speaks to the divine.

They land, grounding, a reminder of reality's pull.
Dialogue between past and future, held together by sweat and
    beats.
Their body sways, twists, and turns, sometimes frenetic,
sometimes with the relaxed grace of wisdom.
Then, as the crescendo builds, a moment of stillness—

a poignant pause that speaks more than words.
It's in this silence the dance's essence is most felt, a quiet space
where understanding blooms, connections are forged.
They begin again, a flurry of movement, a culmination

of journeys, a declaration of being. Each step a testament
to years of discipline and passion and parts never fully healed.
Yet just as the crescendo seems imminent, the music halts.
The theater plunges into startled silence.

The dancer's body stills. The emotion does not wane.
It shifts, becoming a force reaching out, yearning.
The dancer's arm stretches forward, fingers quivering,
seeking, reaching out to the audience as if beckoning
for a kindred spirit. A sea of faces stare back.

From the depths of the audience, a lone hand raises.
The dancer's fingers grasp the hand, and the pull is consuming.
Attached to eyes wide, the hand and the legs are gently
    ushered
onto the stage. The divide between performer and observer
    blurred.
For a moment, the room holds its breath. The dancer, with a
    tenderness,
demonstrates a move. The former observer hesitates,
but finds the courage to mirror it. Another move follows,
and again it is imitated. With each step, a connection deepens,
an unspoken conversation blossoms. The music resumes, its
    rhythm

matching what's unfolding on stage. The synergy between the
    dancer
and the once-passive observer is electric. Emboldened, the
    dancer reaches out again,
inviting another from the audience. And then another—until
    the stage fills,
a rainbow of individuals. As the energy swells, a beautiful
    chaos
ensues, others reach out, drawing more and more from the
    audience, hoping
to share the experience. The boundaries shattered, the
    distinction
between performer and observer dissolves.

[With that, the final notes lingered, the dancers' silhouettes faded into the darkness, and the theater was once again awash in the soft hum of voices, until someone began playing music from their phone and yelled, "Let's take the party outside!"]

C.R.E.A.M.

"Cash rules—
Word up, two for fives over here, baby

Cash rules everything—
Word up, two for fives, niggas got garbage down the way

Cash rules everything around—
Word up, know what I'm sayin'?"

Capitalism's mantra, like scurrying mice
heard through tenement walls,
dollar-dollar bill y'all. The song of sirens chasing
ghosts of those hustling away a lifetime on corners
of hugged blocks where their mommas rent.

Bloody, crisp and green, folded into paper bullets,
stitched into the lining of coats that will end
up in evidence lockers, after arguments over
who gets more zeros, not realizing everyone is a loser.

Lies found at the bottom of overpriced bottles,
section of the club flooding with steel-filled rage,
erasing promises to get momma out.

Bloody, crumbled, and green, fished from pockets
of a red sea, to silence the hum of cash registers,
no care for momma losing the best part of her day.
Cash rules everything around me.

Stumbling through Self-Care

In the emptiness where depression sleeps, I washed
my grief down with a chianti-dark river,
its bitter currents singing me into numbness.
I raised a toast to the starless sky, my glass
a mausoleum of denial, reflecting
only what I wished to see.

I wore the music like a second skin,
let it vibrate through my bones,
tried to shake the sadness away,
dancing with the shadows of dust left behind.

I sought solace in the twist of my curls,
hoping my own reflection would morph
into someone I don't remember.

What few coins I had, I tossed in the air,
wishing on each as it fell, until the balance ran crimson,
debt blooming like roses on my credit card.

I unknotted love from my life,
hoping for solace in solitude,
believing that a lonely heart heals quicker.
It still clung to me: a bitter cologne in the summer heat.
Then I outran the sun, crossing borders,
but melancholy claimed me in every time zone.

In the circles of busyness, I ran,
whirling dervish, spinning out of control,
became as dizzying as what was within—
my world, a blur.

Passed over Petals

Like the marigold beginning to bloom in summer's glow,

Petals trembling with nervous excitement,

Yearning to be plucked from the crowd, I declare—

Here I am! Wishing to be seen,

For eyes to marvel at the delicacy of my existence,

The strength in my tender roots. To be chosen.

But I am tossed glances, like coins into a beggar's cup,

Fleeting seconds of inspection rather than investment.

There is peace in the passersby,

The silence that settles after their departure,

Space birthed from my name unsaid. Serenity being unseen.

Slowly blossoming only for the sky, and freedom

Found in the mirror. I have learned glances

Are not the sun, and touch is not rain.

At the Edge of Eternity

In the quiet, you are there.
Your breath: a secret on the edge of sound
dancing in the wind's whispers. A keepsake
of a voice that sings to me. A reminder:
atoms do not surrender to death.
Instead, they waltz beyond and with us,
a ballet of constancy woven through the fabric of time.
Our harmonies exist in the silence between heartbeats,
Here, now, cradled in the past's palm,
flowing to the ear of the future.
At the end, as in the beginning,
our atoms remain undefeated.

If You Are Not an Ocean

Then explain
How too much of you
Feels like drowning
But too little of us
Leaves me lifeless,
Longing for depth's pull,
Balance of our shared drift.

Session III: To Eulogize a Man

Rage once carved its home in the chambers of a man.
Boyhood pillars, barbed and tangled, became a cruel
    foundation.
I navigated the fortress of this binary, my heart under rusted
    lock.
My tears untold myths in the hollow of my eyes.

Can you see the tyrant's sword I carried,
Masculine rigidness engraved, bloomed from roots
Rotting in ancient deceit?

But the Reaper's ledger bore my name.
In the way of a reckoning,
Cast naked into the underbelly of moonlight,
Beneath the shroud of the world's oldest mother,
I died—and then I became

A man, not by the measure of years,
But by the weight of choices fossilized within my marrow.

A cemetery of selves, quiet within
Unmarked graves, housing faces I once wore.
Buried in the alcoves of memory,
Rabid ghosts gnawed at the peace of those
Who loved me.

Shall we gather tonight, in the ghost light?
So you might help me write the eulogy
For the people I once was.

No roses, no tears, just the quiet ritual
Of acknowledging the truth,
And letting it rest in the land of yesterday.
I nurture new seeds watered
with accountability wrung from my past selves.

IV.

The Sherman Cabin

I rest my weary bones

Made of calcium, front lines, and prayer

Painfully bent, crooked, contorted

Yet remaining arced toward freedom

A sigh of relief

As the weight of the world

Slips from my shoulders

Into calloused hands

To be placed on a nightstand

If only for a day, morning, hour

So I might pick up a book

Or scotch a toast to surviving

A drink to those who did not

Sonnet of the Skin

I.

In this America, in this theater of unending trials,
I know we were born into this geography of wounds,
But hush now, mind. Be still, heart, please.

In the silent embrace of midnight, the body transforms into a ship, meticulously crafted by an artist's trembling hand, humming a tune laden with unease. This vessel's blueprint reveals a tempestuous heart—a storm coursing through veins, the passionate twirl of a soul bearing scars. It's in this profound stillness that heartbeats echo with the intensity of djembe drummers, and anxious fingertips chart pathways of worry, all cascading toward an unknown abyss.

It's not through fault of ours,
but a consequence of our pigment:
a mark of an ancestral sun.
They don't see the stories beneath our skin,
nor the blood that sighs in our veins,
that are as much roots,
as they are middle passage ripples.

II.

A prayer woven in electric shock, twitching beneath the sternum, a plucked string vibrating in the hollow of my throat, playing an arrangement no one requested. Every breath is a fight, an intimate quarrel between lungs and air. Each inhale a trespasser in the crimson chambers of life's rhythm. Each exhale: a reluctant surrender.

Yes, Uncle Sam scorched us with his gaze,
but remember how we shimmered under sun's dominion,
Carved from oak and iron, we are a history, a memory,
a love song whispered in dark fields beneath an old sky.

III.

The world distorts itself through the lens of a trembling iris—stretching and contracting, dilating into a feverish blur. People, places, moments—all become ill-defined shadows against the stark-white curtain of panic, their forms melting into an abstract soup of fear and confusion.

True, affirmative action may be no more.
The noose may hide in plain sight,
but are we not under the watchful eyes of those strange fruits?
Even within this chaos, under this concrete rain,
our bodies are an atlas, bearing the weight of Black futures.

IV.

There is a forest in my veins growing with the intensity of a wild, unchecked summer. The trees sway with the gale of my pulse: a tempest that refuses to still their leaves shimmering in the moonlight of adrenaline—rustling, whispering their disquiet. I am the lone traveler in this lush labyrinth. No breadcrumbs to guide me home.

Oh, I know how the pandemic laid siege to our lungs,
and the burning forests in Canada don't help.
Ancestors laid low before their time,
all while we marched for George Floyd,
met with the brazen lash of baton,

and the cold kiss of handcuffs.
But aren't we more than the scars they gave?

V.

In the grip of this terror, my skin becomes a sonnet—each pore an unstated metaphor for a fear that has no name, each hair standing at attention, a line in the tragic poem of my body's revolt. The ghost of the panic attack stalks me, each footprint echoing louder than the last, a nocturnal ballet scored by the orchestra of my body.

I'm moved by the aftershock of gavels falling,
and my ears also bleed from the wailing of sirens,
the badges, the blue, the cries in the night,
videos too grotesque, verdicts too mild, a system unyielding.
Yet we are more than the sum of their sins.

VI.

There is a paradox in the crescendo of anxiety, for even as I drown, I am aflame. A pyre in the ocean, each wave both quenching and kindling—my fear and my defense in a bewildering waltz. In the stuttering lamplight of this internal chaos, I am a lighthouse to no one, a beacon consumed by its own beam.

I wish I could carry your burden of bearing witness
in a world that often squints at the sun of confrontation.
They won't give you your flowers until you're gone.
Yet within you, a fortitude forged in the fires of trials.
But what would there be to dance to
if we didn't have your drumbeat of survival and defiance?

VII.

But still, amid the throbbing disarray, a bloom of resilience, tenacious as dawn breaking the night. This dissonance, this cacophony, it may wound but it does not vanquish. The body knows its rhythm, the heart, its staccato song. Amid the tempest's roar, there exists a melody of survival, a harmony carved into the marrow, tuned by the strum of living.

Let's count backwards from ten.

In Another Life

For Porsche Joseph

When my pulse fades,
I'll chase the silhouette of you swaying
To music, knowing our song is next to play.
And if I can no longer see or hear,
I'll follow the scent of your perfume,
Knowing the sweetness of your skin.
Through the doors where time is hushed,
I'll search for the trail of your laughter,
Tracing it back to the moment we met,
When I first held the horizon line of your hands,
Rested in the sanctuary of your voice.
When my breath grows thin,
Find me waiting for you on a street
Lined with magnolias, unchanged in essence,
And yet new. You'll know it's me as you walk closer.
Listen for the sound of my heart skipping a beat.

1520 Sedgwick Avenue

For J Dilla and Hip Hop

A box of my mother's old cassette tapes—
that's where I met hip hop.
Not as a name, but a movement,
a heart-thud, dancing
against my body's thick skin.

It was not music, but rather
a rapture, a rolling thunder,
a language born from streets I knew,
and the souls of those
who dared to speak when the world
didn't want to listen.

It was rhythm and rhyme,
stories of struggle and time,
of lives lived in the shadows,
of dreams bigger than project buildings,
from voices filled with poetry and pain.

From the bronze gates of a Sony Walkman,
sounds, boisterous and brash,
I remember the beat,
how it flowed through me,
like blood, like breath,
like a river that knew no end,
like Whitman or Dickinson could never.

Stories by asphalt-birthed prophets,
head nodding beats and bars,
808s banging life into my marrow,
in loops, and lies, and truths,
I thought only my neighborhood knew.

And in that moment,
I understood what it meant
to be alive, to be a part of something
greater than myself,
a revolution of human spirit.

What a Difference a Day Made

She stood at the edge of our shared silence.
It was morning, but the long night was draped over her.
Against my better judgment, I crossed the room,
Heart racing with the wild of our last fight.
Unsure whether it was raining or her gaze was a storm.
I wanted to say something,
But had no voice, and even if I did,
We didn't speak the same language anymore.
Inhaling our crumbling world. I said, *I still love you—*
As if we weren't the architects of our own heartbreak,
And arsonists, and masochists, and archnemeses, and best
   friends.
I couldn't let her go. But the wounds had never been soft
   enough
To heal without time. Apart. Strangers. Faces in the crowd.
There's no other way to save a life.

Session IV: Tina's Cups

In November 1993, the CDC reported that HIV became the leading cause of death for African American men ages twenty-five to forty-four and the second leading cause of death for African American women in the same age range.

I often consider the weight of your cups
cradled in the limbo of those years,

learning to bear an uninvited guest
ravaging the village of your immune system,

struggling to find places to still love you.
Cups you'd sip from in silence, always the same two,

rims grazing lips consciously. Never in my grasp.
The resilience with which they'd ascend to your lips

despite not knowing when or if there would be an answer.
I think of them lying empty at night,

of the porcelain whispering your truth,
or anchoring you in the eye of the storm.

All the things they saw you face subtly, steadily,
slimming to the sternest reality. Keeping your secrets.

How they resonated with you. What they wouldn't let
you become, in the absence of HAART or PEP.

Held in the hand or resting on the edge of our lips.
I tried to decide what they conveyed when they woke up

and discovered someone else was near.
Don't touch those! you said, pushing further the stark silence

between us. My favorite cousin, withering away. Into the void
of your battle that everyone was losing.

The rest of the family said they didn't know why my mother
let you stay:
She got that Magic Johnson. Don't touch anything she touches,

and hold your breath when she walks by. Practicing fear like
scripture.
But my mother watched the news, and my mother read the
books,

and my mother could have become a scientist, because my
mother loved you
like you were her own. She wasn't going to let her niece fight
alone,

like your father had to. Even though everyone said it was
cancer when it wasn't.
Because we used to take care of each other, and she
remembered our history.

So she lifted your cup, knowing it held more than water, and
you yelled,

and she yelled, too. You wanted her to live, but she wanted you
   to live, too.

While others stayed ignorant, she drank the truth.
You cried, then she cried, so I cried, too. Neither of you knew

I was there the whole time. But you kept crying, letting us
   know
you appreciated how we had been there the whole time.

Afterwards, your cups returned to the cupboard,
finding a home with the others.

In the Slow Hum of Hindsight

Time thickens like honey, its sweetness cut
With the vinegar tang of absence. I take time
To sit with our loss. To count the cost of the names
On our tongues repeated until they lost form, becoming
Nothing but sound. As I catch my breath long enough
For a glimpse of this society, I see a mirage of lives
That once were. Tears fall as I begin to pluck
Familiar faces from memory, like stones
From a riverbed holding them up to our fractured
Sunlight, examining the shape of their void, not believing
They could be real. When did their smiles become
Sepia photographs bleached by the wilting hours?
We are a world traveling from one pocket
Of silence to another, carrying the weight
Of a million goodbyes settled heavy
As dust on their old furniture.

Guns Don't Weep for Us

the bullets whizzing
through the wind's whispers
a child's innocence silenced

by the thunder of steel.

a mother's heart crumbles,

a father's hands, heavy,

and in the classroom
and on the playground
and at the movie theater
and anywhere a child should be safe
the shadow of the NRA swallows

a generation whole.

tell me, America, which will it be,

the gun or the child?

Tears of a Clown

Under this fading tent we are tattered,
But undeniably whole in memory.
There I search for us, in the sweeping spotlight.
We were bathed in laughter's confetti once—
Weren't we?

Adorned in cotton candy and elephant trumpets.
Mama, do you remember?

Our relationship, now a funhouse mirror,
Bent and twisted in a distortion of what we used to be.
This isn't what we always were.

One way or another, they will place us in a museum,
Beside the Big Top. A photo of a balloon
Tinsel-tied to an anchor—and a trapeze missing its mark,
Leaving our relationship suspended in midair.

On your shoulders, high above the crowd,
I remember our world unbroken,
Within the circus of our past, I still find myself wishing
We would walk the tightrope toward one another.
Unsteady, uncertain, patient.

Where is the woman who held my sticky hands?
Now, barely a spectator in the audience
Of what I have faced. When I need
Your guidance. Now, a night flicker,
In the grandstand of the past,
I search for the mother I once knew.

Looking in the mirror, I can still trace her face,
Finding memories of two acrobats, lost in the act,
Routine grown unfamiliar by rusted unicycle.

An elephant's march is still heavier than silent arguments.
I'd rather words unsaid roar like caged lions,
Yearning to spill out into freedom on the plains.

Yet despite the uncaged beast of resentment,
And unspoken lines in a parent's script,
I still remember you as the safety net below.

I still reach across the gap, hoping
When we are reborn, you'll be there
To catch my fall.

If My Dog Isn't God

What is God if not the dawn that bleeds into the grasp of
     morning,
the songs of cicadas echoing in the summer's heat,
or the taste of the first ripe peaches from a tree you planted?

Does the divine reside in an unseen world,
or could it be nestled in the things that dare to love us
more than we love ourselves?

Found not in grand cathedrals, but in proof of life's purity and
     decentness.
In things unswayed by private jet sermons. Unsullied by stains
     of man's theology.

Does She dwell in distant stars or in familiar hazel twinkles?
In the vastness of space and time, or in the love that fills those
     voids,
rustling of leaves in the wind, or twitching ears toward my
     voice?

What is God, if not the love seen in the celestial dance of a
     tail, soft thuds
like trumpets sounding from heaven's door? A joy so radiant,
     it casts halos
onto the weary-hearted. What is God, if not the wonder

of his hazel eyes gazing upon a fluttering butterfly, echoing
     Eden
in his silent contemplation? What is God, if not the miracles

called my boy's eyes, reflecting me better than I deserve to be
    seen,
peeling away my façade, forgiving without judgment,
loving my most beautiful corners, saving my soul.
If God is not there, then where would She be?

V.

Breathing While Your Therapist Is on Vacation

Now exhale and repeat after me.

On days I'm alive,
A universe blooms in my lungs,
Joy finding home within a body
Once thought a legend, poured from
The cups of the ancestors.

In this country, Black futures are my reason,
Because our freedom is chiseled in the grooves
Of ancient stones. Older than gaslighting texts.

If we were made in his image, then call us by our name.

My light, a gentle lover, touches everything differently,
Inheriting the fire of stars. Crafting my form
With a tenderness reserved for deities,
While the air holds its breath in a moment of reverence
Gathered around me like a poem's blanket, or
Love letters folded into my pocket since birth.

I am only invisible to those who see with mortal eyes.
But if you're looking, find me like the solitary dandelion
Dancing in the gales, each gust a kiss from full lips.

The first one placed on my big forehead—
Just like my momma's.
The next placed on my wide nose—
Just like her momma's.

There I will be navigating chaos, vibrancy,
Filth and fervor. Finding myself no longer a stranger
In the anthems of the living, a paper character sprung
From someone else's imagination,
Cast adrift in the waters of absence and confusion.

I am a continent, known in the language of my foremothers
    and fathers
Yelling on the edge of forever until hope is truth:

We alive, beloved!

To Silver Strands

Each a token of wisdom earned,

A testament to years well spent.

Because they were mine.

My body, less agile than the day before,

now tells stories, of the roads I've traveled,

the battles I've fought. Forehead creases carved

by laughter and sorrow, a map of memories

etched into every groove.

My limbs may creak now, my pace may slow,

But age has stolen nothing. I am blessed

With a knowing face, and songs

Of all I have experienced.

I've seen the sunset's fire, and dawn's embrace.

Though the tempo changes, the rhythm shifts,

Still I dance. So let these strands multiply.

My badges of honor,

Reminders that I have lived, and loved,

And grown in the fertile soil of time.

An Unhurried Love

My losses have been too complicated
For my sort of love not to be kept simple.

In it, I am but a child,
Dancing in the midst of a summer's rain,
Tracing adventures on fogged windows.

My sort of love is soothing, like the brook
Behind my childhood home.
Loud enough to always find my way back.

It is a native tongue, speaking to me as trees do,
Unscripted, in the embrace of a single note,
Held long and near.

My sort of love whispers unhurried vows,
Tenderly pulling me over and over
Into the gravity of the sunrise.

Tyre and His Skateboard

In memoriam: Tyre Nichols 1993–2023

Dearest Tyre, where are you now?

May your skateboard be with you.

For joy is what I hope is left after loss.

With concrete beneath your wheels,

You are more than a victim of circumstance.

A symphony of motion and sound

Drowns out hate where you are.

Ride with purpose!

Turn and leap to your heart's content!

You are not bound to anything.

The thrill of being free

And the wind kissing your face.

We Can't Forget

How to sing, barefoot on the dew-kissed grass,
lost in the gravity of ourselves.

Holding yesterday close.
Eyes turned from the vastness

of tomorrow. We are as young
as the last word to leave our lips,
as young as the last light
trapped in our eyes.

There are lifetimes carved out
in the pomegranate pulse of our hearts.

The Weight of Every Bite

Poverty can make you unsure
That you even enjoy food.

Who has McDonald's money
When there is food at home?

Make a plate at your Aunt's house
Because mommy isn't cooking later,

And you better eat it all, even though you're full.
Can't leave the table until you do.

Have you thought about kids in Africa?
World's weight on the edge of your fork.

When you stop overdrafting enough to enjoy
The art of a marbled steak and a glass of Pinot.

There is barely a need for cutlery, just fingers.
Tender morsels awakening something primal.

Hunger, once a cage, now becomes a passport.

I Remembered What Living Is

As I sat in the park folded in the lap
of a cotton candy sky, shadow of the city resting
on my shoulders, and the grass green
as a spring memory, inviting me
to let go, to breathe, to be.

I closed my eyes and was cradled,
like a baby, like a bird, like an open book.

I became a melody, a lyric of the grass,
a hymn of the city birds. Oh, those city birds,
with their concrete chirps and steel-feathered songs.

The chorus was a question, "Are you simply alive or living?"
Loud as a lover's laughter, subtle as a sigh.
I wore my day in the park like an heirloom,
gifting my skin the healing sun.
I don't want to be an interlude in my own existence.

Flights to Essence Fest

Nestled between the hush-hum of engines
And the extension of silk-covered dreams,
Where gravity is but a tease. It's here:
The Black woman sits, cocooned in metal and sky,
Held together by childlike anticipation.

A pilgrimage of liberation, where she isn't asked
To be mother, wife, sister, daughter, friend,
Election saver, chef, shoulder, educator,
Intersectionalist, or mythical.

Where she isn't asked to spin the world,
To carry its weight, its woes, but to release,
Let loose her laughter, like the luxury
She has given to flocks
Of those she brought into sunrise.

No room for anything but herself at thirty-thousand feet,
Treated not as the storm, but the rainbow it promises.
Does America offer her a freer moment than this?

If There Is a God Who Listens

Was it you who unburdened my sunken shoulders?

Pulled me from the depths,
Where I was submerged
In a turbulent sea—
A duel with inner tides—

Lifted weights not mine to bear,
Nudged me past unseen perils?
There, shadows hungry, ready to consume.

When I was willing to be the lamb,
Was it you who kept me from wilting,
Offering another path,
In lands I thought fit for my end?

Always ahead, filling the abyss,
Unshackling chains I wrongfully claim,
Drowning me in compassion's flood,
Igniting memories of innocence, days gone by.

Every tremble, every plea,
Whenever I wander, lost in the night,
Collecting each tear, each sigh,
Forming a river, guiding me back,
So I might find my way home.

Was it you?

Our Birthright

Before the robin sings to the sunrise,
There's a ritual touch on the nape of my neck,
Fingers on the braille of ink, four letters,
Bound to faith like a prayer humming on the skin.

It reads *love*, a trailing note from grandmother's lips,
The keepsake from a matriarch's final gift,
Before being called home to her kin.
Mother, sister, son, familiar laughs,
And shared sorrow. She's there now,
Never too far but still beyond my reach.

She said, *that word should be a birthright*,
But for us, it's often a hard-fought war.
Our folk don't win it shedding blood,
We win it givin' what we lookin' fo.

That's what her great-grandfather once said.
Who had won his war toiling in the soil
Of a Carolina plantation, while asking the sun
Why Jesus didn't love him.

It spoke to him in the passed down language of seeds,
Earned in the West African tradition of being tender
With what we touch. In return, the Earth spilled
forth generous laughter in the form of ripe,
blushing tomatoes. Where massa could not see.
It's okay. Eat, child.

The Colors Worth Seeing

What could be more beautiful
Than a child in the bathroom's half-light,
Eyes wide, confronting the mirror—
Pressing a kiss to that rainbow reflection?
Beyond loud lies, past the door's timber,
They find themselves.

Trembling with the excitement of eulogizing
Dead names and old expectations.

Like pearls released from a tightly clasped necklace,
What gathers in the corners of that freeing?

When their laughter rings louder than anger of parents
Who claimed to love them regardless.
Like a melody escaping a songbird's imagination,
What blossoms in the space their delight inhabits?

And later, when they lay on a bed of blossoms,
What relentless wonder might be born of these petals?

Acknowledgments

To you, the luminous wanderer who continues to journey with me,

The world as we know it is in constant flux, like waves crashing and retreating, and each morning brings a mystery that even the bravest hearts can't predict. Yet here we are, in this sacred present, finding what's worth fighting for. We are often armed with nothing but the will to protect what brings light to our souls—which will always be enough.

Thank you for sharing this path with me, for letting my words be a small part of your life. It is an honor, a gift beyond measure, to be in your company as we navigate the unknown together.

To Porsche,

In the tender labyrinths of every verse I've penned, in the whispered pause between each word, there you are—a heart beating through the narrative of my life. You've illuminated the darkened corners of my thoughts, pulling my voice from the shadows when it trembled in hesitance. I love you.

To V,

It's a tall task to build a monument with a stranger. In the spaces between ink and intent, where words tremble on the ledge of becoming and unbecoming, there you were—helping sculpt notes into symphony. Thank you for approaching my words as wild, living things, deserving of both reverence and understanding.

To my dearest friends,

When shadows whispered that I am unworthy of tenderness, you wrapped me in the truest form of the word. When the world pronounced me unlovable, you loved me enough for all the lifetimes we have been friends.

Thank you. Not just for being there, but for reminding me that friendship, true friendship, is both an anchor and a sail. With all of you, I have felt both held and free.

To Michael,

Whose departure from this world has left us with a void no words can fill, yet whose spirit continues to light our path in the darkness. You were a fortress of compassion, and a direction toward hope in a world often too comfortable with despair. In every room you entered, you made space not just for yourself, but for all those whose voices had been silenced by history's cruel hand. You understood, perhaps better than most, that our work is not to simply create art, but to create possibility—a chance for healing, for progress, for equity to take root and flourish in the soils of our collective soul. This poetry collection, and our shared hope for it, will forever speak to your legacy, brother. It will be a testament to your work for a future where love and justice are not just ideals, but realities. You will not be defined by your absence, but by what you did with your time here. Rest now, knowing the efforts continue, and through us, you are forever. And as promised, I will eventually still go on a silent retreat.

The Michael Latt Legacy Fund is dedicated to supporting artists from underrepresented communities, leveraging storytelling for enduring impact, bringing diverse communities together, and building opportunities that focus on equity and positive change. To use art to foster love, hope, and healing.

To learn more and support, visit: http://michaellattlegacy.com.